Woman Evolve
THE WORKBOOK

Disclaimer:
This workbook provides general information and personal perspectives. It is not a substitute for professional advice, counseling, or therapy. Seek guidance from qualified professionals for specific issues. Use discretion when applying the content and take responsibility for your decisions. Your unique situation may require individualized support.

LESSONS IN THIS WORKBOOK:

Chapter 1: Breaking Up with Fear

Chapter 2: Identity Crisis

Chapter 3: Beauty in the Broken

Chapter 4: Ugly Beautiful

Chapter 5: When Forgiveness Meets Accountability

Chapter 6: Black Women's Superpower

Chapter 7: Love in the Layers

Chapter 8: The Great Envy

Chapter 9: Leaving Pieces Behind

Chapter 10: Revolutionizing Your Life

Chapter 1: Breaking Up with Fear

Facing Your Fears: Sarah Jakes Roberts passionately drives home the idea that it's vital to not only acknowledge your fears but to confront them directly. Often, we tend to sweep our fears under the rug or pretend they don't exist, but this approach can hinder our personal growth. By looking fear in the eye, you gain a profound insight into what's been holding you back.

Fear as a Formidable Obstacle: This chapter vividly illustrates how fear often stands as a formidable obstacle in the way of realizing your true potential. It's that voice that tells you not to pursue your dreams, avoid taking risks, and stay within your comfort zone. Understanding how fear limits your actions and choices is a crucial first step in the journey toward breaking free from its grasp.

Embracing the Power of Courage: With infectious enthusiasm, Sarah encourages her readers to embrace courage as a mighty weapon against fear. Courage doesn't mean you won't feel afraid; rather, it's the audacity to take action despite those fears. By nurturing a sense of courage within yourself, you're equipped to challenge your fears head-on and make choices that propel you toward personal growth and profound transformation.

As you delve further into this chapter, anticipate encountering personal stories, engaging exercises, and uplifting anecdotes. Sarah Jakes Roberts masterfully weaves these elements together to illustrate the lessons and ignite a fire within you to kickstart your own fearless journey. The ultimate mission? To empower women like you to step into their full potential and lead lives unburdened by fear. This chapter sets the stage for a captivating exploration of self-discovery, self-acceptance, and the magnificent journey of personal transformation that lies ahead. Get ready to break up with your fears and revolutionize your life!

Write down three fears that have been holding you back in life.

_____

_____

_____

_____

_____

_____

_____

_____

_____

_____

_____

_____

_____

_____

_____

_____

_____

_____

_____

_____

_____

_____

_____

_____

_____

_____

_____

Describe a specific situation where you successfully confronted and overcame a fear.

_____

_____

_____

_____

_____

_____

_____

_____

_____

_____

_____

_____

_____

_____

_____

_____

_____

_____

_____

_____

_____

_____

_____

_____

_____

_____

List three actionable steps you can take to start confronting your fears.

_____

_____

_____

_____

_____

_____

_____

_____

Confronting your _____ is essential for personal growth.

To propel your life forward, you must _____ your fears directly.

Identify and address the _____ that are holding you back.

Overcoming fear requires taking _____ action.

True or False: Confronting fears is not necessary for personal growth.

True or False: Facing fears head-on can lead to personal transformation.

True or False: Avoiding fears is the best way to handle them.

True or False: Taking action despite fear is a sign of courage.

Lesson 2:

Recognize that fear can be a major roadblock to unlocking your true potential.

Reflect on a time when fear held you back from pursuing a goal or dream.

_____

_____

_____

_____

_____

_____

_____

_____

_____

_____

_____

_____

_____

_____

_____

_____

_____

_____

_____

_____

_____

_____

_____

_____

_____

_____

_____

_____

Write down the ways in which fear has limited your actions and choices in the past.

_____

_____

_____

_____

_____

_____

_____

_____

_____

_____

_____

_____

_____

_____

_____

_____

_____

_____

_____

_____

_____

_____

_____

_____

_____

_____

Share a personal experience of someone you know who overcame fear and unlocked their potential.

_____

_____

_____

_____

_____

_____

_____

_____

Cloze Tests:

Fear can act as a significant _____ to reaching your true potential.

Recognizing the impact of fear is the first step toward _____ your potential.

List some ways in which fear has _____ your choices.

Overcoming fear can lead to unlocking your _____ potential.

True/False Exercises:

True or False: Fear has no impact on one's potential.

True or False: Recognizing the influence of fear is the first step toward growth.

True or False: Fear always encourages taking risks.

True or False: Overcoming fear is not related to unlocking one's true potential.

Lesson 3:

Embrace courage as a mighty tool to liberate yourself from the clutches of fear.

Describe a situation where you acted courageously despite feeling fear.

List three ways in which courage can help you break free from fear.

_____

_____

_____

_____

_____

_____

_____

_____

_____

_____

_____

_____

_____

_____

_____

_____

_____

_____

_____

_____

_____

_____

_____

_____

Reflect on the difference between courage and fearlessness.
Share a personal story of someone you admire who exemplified
courage in their life.

_____

_____

_____

_____

_____

_____

_____

_____

_____

_____

_____

_____

Courage is a powerful tool to _____ yourself from fear.
Acting courageously means taking action despite feeling

_____.

Courage empowers you to _____ the clutches of fear.
Fearlessness is not the same as _____.
True/False Exercises:
True or False: Courage has no impact on overcoming fear.
True or False: Acting courageously means being completely
without fear.
True or False: Courage can empower you to break free from fear.
True or False: Fearlessness and courage are synonymous.

Chapter 2: Identity Crisis

Let's dive into Chapter 2 of "Woman Evolve: Break Up with Your Fears and Revolutionize Your Life" by Sarah Jakes Roberts. In this chapter, we're going on an exciting journey to uncover the power of our identity and how it shapes our lives.

First up, Sarah Jakes Roberts encourages us to embark on an epic adventure of self-discovery. Imagine it like setting sail on a voyage to explore the vast ocean of your own identity. This adventure involves some deep introspection and self-reflection. You'll be asking yourself big questions about who you truly are, what makes you tick, your beliefs, values, passions, and your wildest dreams. Understanding your identity isn't just important; it's like finding the treasure map to personal growth and fulfillment!

Next, we're getting real about self-worth. Many of us grapple with feelings of not being "enough" or self-doubt. Sarah's here to tell us that we're all stars in our own right. Picture this: you're a shining diamond in a world full of gems. You don't need anyone else's approval or validation to sparkle. Self-acceptance is our secret weapon, and it's high time we wield it proudly.

And here's the grand finale of this chapter: discovering how our identity influences our life choices. Think of your identity as your North Star, guiding you on your life's journey. It's like having a personal GPS that helps you make decisions. Sarah's going to show us how the beliefs and perceptions we hold about ourselves impact every choice we make. From the job you take to the people you surround yourself with, your identity plays a starring role in your life story.

Chapter Explanation (Detailed):

In this electrifying Chapter 2, Sarah Jakes Roberts invites us to join her on an extraordinary quest of self-discovery and self-acceptance. It's like strapping into a rocket and launching into the cosmos of who you are.

We start by peeling back the layers to uncover our true identity. It's a bit like peering into the depths of your soul and finding treasure hidden within. Who are you at your core? What do you believe in? What are your passions and dreams? These are the questions we'll be answering on this adventure. Knowing yourself is like holding the key to a treasure chest filled with personal growth and fulfillment.

But that's not all! Sarah is our enthusiastic guide, reminding us that each of us is unique and inherently valuable. Imagine yourself as the brightest star in the night sky, not needing anyone else's affirmation to shine. Self-acceptance is our superpower, and Sarah's here to teach us how to wield it like a pro.

Now, picture your identity as your trusty co-pilot on the journey of life. It's like having your personal navigation system, guiding you through every twist and turn. The decisions you make, from your career to your relationships, are all influenced by this identity GPS. Sarah's going to show us how understanding this connection empowers us to make choices that align with our true selves.

Write down five adjectives that describe your personality.

_____

_____

_____

_____

_____

_____

_____

_____

_____

_____

_____

_____

Describe a moment in your life when you felt most connected to your true self.

_____

_____

_____

_____

_____

_____

_____

_____

_____

_____

_____

_____

_____

_____

_____

_____

_____

_____

_____

_____

_____

_____

_____

_____

_____

_____

List three core values that are important to you.

_____

_____

_____

_____

_____

Cloze Tests:
Exploring your sense of _____ is essential for self-discovery.
Self-worth is not dependent on _____ approval.
Identify at least three of your core _____.
External _____ should not determine your self-worth.
True/False Exercises:
True or False: Self-discovery is not important for personal growth.
True or False: Self-worth is solely determined by external valida-
tion.
True or False: Your personality traits can be described with adjec-
tives.
True or False: Core values are not relevant to one's identity.

Lesson 2:

Recognize the importance of self-discovery and self-acceptance.

Share a personal experience of when self-discovery led to personal growth.

_____

_____

_____

_____

_____

_____

_____

_____

_____

_____

_____

_____

_____

_____

_____

_____

_____

_____

_____

_____

_____

_____

_____

_____

_____

_____

_____

_____

_____

Write down three things you appreciate about yourself.

Describe a situation where self-acceptance helped you overcome a challenge. List three steps you can take to further explore and accept your true self.

_____

_____

_____

_____

_____

_____

_____

_____

_____

_____

_____

Cloze Tests:
Self-discovery is a crucial step toward personal _____.
Recognizing your strengths and weaknesses is part of self-

_____.
Self-acceptance means embracing yourself with all your

_____.
Exploring and accepting your true self is an ongoing _____.
True/False Exercises:
True or False: Self-discovery has no impact on personal growth.
True or False: Self-acceptance means ignoring your weaknesses.
True or False: Recognizing your strengths is a part of self-discovery.
True or False: Exploring and accepting your true self is a one-time process.

Lesson 3:

Understand how your identity impacts your life choices.

Describe a decision you made that was influenced by your self-perception.

List three ways in which your identity has influenced your career choices.

_____

_____

_____

_____

_____

_____

_____

_____

_____

_____

_____

_____

_____

_____

_____

_____

_____

_____

_____

_____

_____

_____

_____

_____

_____

_____

Reflect on how your beliefs about yourself affect your relationships. Share a personal story of a time when aligning your choices with your true self led to positive outcomes.

_____

_____

_____

_____

_____

_____

_____

_____

_____

_____

Cloze Tests:

Your identity acts as your personal _____ system for life choices.

Beliefs about yourself can impact your _____ and relationships.

Making choices aligned with your true self can lead to _____ outcomes.

Your identity plays a significant role in shaping your life _____.

True/False Exercises:

True or False: Your identity has no influence on your life choices.

True or False: Beliefs about yourself have no impact on your relationships.

True or False: Aligning choices with your true self can lead to positive outcomes.

True or False: Your identity is irrelevant to your life story.

Chapter 3: Beauty in the Broken

Jumping into Chapter 3 of "Woman Evolve: Break Up with Your Fears and Revolution-ize Your Life" by Sarah Jakes Roberts. In this chapter, we're on a thrilling mission to unearth the strength and beauty hidden within our vulnerabilities and past experiences.

First up, Sarah Jakes Roberts encourages us to flex our vulnerability muscles. Imagine vulnerability as a superpower waiting to be unleashed, not a weakness. By owning our flaws and sharing our struggles, we connect with our true selves and build resilience like superheroes.

Now, get ready for a mind-blowing idea: your past doesn't have a say in your future! Sarah's here to challenge the status quo and declare that your history doesn't have to write your destiny. No matter the challenges or blunders you've faced, you're the author of your own story. It's like getting a fresh canvas to paint your dream life.

Brace yourself for the grand finale – transforming your brokenness into growth. Imag-ine your life's challenges and setbacks as stepping stones on the path to your best self. Instead of dwelling on the pain, Sarah invites us to see these experiences as opportuni-ties for learning, healing, and personal development.

Chapter Explanation (Detailed):

Chapter 3, "Beauty in the Broken," is a thrilling adventure into the heart of our vulnera-bilities and past experiences, where we'll discover hidden strengths and the potential for transformation.

Sarah Jakes Roberts kicks things off by encouraging us to embrace vulnerability as a superpower. Instead of treating it as a weakness, she wants us to wield it like a weapon of courage. Imagine vulnerability as the secret sauce that connects us to our true selves and builds up our inner resilience. It's like unlocking a hidden treasure chest of strength.

Now, here's the plot twist: your past doesn't get to call the shots for your future! Sarah passionately challenges the notion that your history writes your destiny. No matter what obstacles, mistakes, or pain you've faced in the past, she's giving you the authority to grab the pen and rewrite your story. It's like being handed a blank canvas where you're the artist, and your dreams are the masterpiece.

But the real showstopper is the concept of turning your brokenness into growth. Imag-ine life's challenges as stepping stones on your journey to becoming the best version of yourself. Instead of dwelling on the tough times, Sarah wants us to view them as opportunities for growth, healing, and personal development. It's like flipping the script and seeing each setback as a setup for a comeback.

Share a vulnerable experience from your past and describe how it made you stronger.

List three qualities or strengths that have emerged from your past challenges.

Reflect on how sharing your vulnerabilities with someone you trust has positively impacted your relationship. Describe a time when you felt empowered by embracing your flaws and vulnerabilities.

_____

_____

_____

_____

_____

_____

_____

_____

_____

_____

Cloze Tests:
Vulnerability can be a source of hidden _____.
Sharing your struggles can help you build _____.
Embracing your _____ can lead to personal growth.
Strength and _____ can emerge from past experiences.
True/False Exercises:
True or False: Vulnerability is a sign of weakness.
True or False: Sharing your struggles doesn't impact your personal growth.
True or False: Embracing your flaws can lead to greater strength.
True or False: Strength and beauty can't emerge from past challenges.

Lesson 2:

Embrace the idea that your past does not define your future.

Write down a past mistake or setback and describe how it has not determined your future.

List three goals or aspirations you have for your future that are not limited by your past.

_____

_____

_____

_____

_____

_____

_____

_____

_____

_____

_____

_____

_____

_____

_____

_____

_____

_____

_____

_____

_____

_____

_____

_____

_____

_____

_____

_____

Reflect on a time when you defied expectations and broke free from your past limitations. Share a personal story of someone you admire who transformed their future despite a challenging past.

_____

_____

_____

_____

_____

_____

_____

_____

_____

Cloze Tests:

Your past doesn't have the power to dictate your _____.

Setting new _____ can break free from past limitations.

Defying expectations can lead to a _____ future.

Transformation is possible regardless of a challenging

_____.

True/False Exercises:

True or False: Your past determines your future.

True or False: Setting new goals can't help break free from past limitations.

True or False: Transformation is not possible if you have a challenging past.

True or False: Defying expectations can lead to a brighter future.

Lesson 3:

Use your brokenness as a source of transformation and growth.

Describe a challenging experience from your past that ultimately
led to personal growth.

List three lessons you've learned from overcoming adversity.

_____

_____

_____

_____

_____

_____

_____

_____

_____

_____

_____

_____

_____

_____

_____

_____

_____

_____

_____

_____

_____

_____

_____

_____

_____

_____

_____

_____

Reflect on how your perspective on setbacks has changed over time. Share a personal story of someone you know who turned their brokenness into a source of strength.

_____

_____

_____

_____

_____

_____

_____

_____

_____

_____

Cloze Tests:

Challenging experiences can be catalysts for _____ and growth.

Overcoming adversity often leads to valuable _____.

Your perspective on setbacks can evolve with _____.

Turning brokenness into strength is a powerful form of

_____.

True/False Exercises:

True or False: Challenging experiences hinder personal growth.

True or False: Overcoming adversity rarely leads to valuable lessons.

True or False: Your perspective on setbacks remains constant over time.

True or False: Turning brokenness into strength is not a powerful transformation.

Chapter 4: Ugly Beautiful

Get ready for Chapter 4 in "Woman Evolve: Break Up with Your Fears and Revolutionize Your Life" by Sarah Jakes Roberts! This chapter is all about diving into the exciting concept of "ugly beautiful" and how it applies to life's challenges.

First things first, let's talk about "ugly beautiful." Sarah Jakes Roberts introduces us to this eye-opening idea that encourages us to find beauty in the midst of life's toughest challenges and difficulties. It's like putting on a new pair of glasses that help us see hidden elements of beauty and growth, even in the most challenging moments.

Brace yourself for the beauty that emerges from adversity! This chapter inspires us to fully embrace the notion that beauty can actually spring forth from difficult situations. While adversity might bring some pain and discomfort, it's also a powerful catalyst for transformation and positive change. Sarah's here to guide us in seeking out the silver linings and valuable lessons within adversity.

Hold on to your hats because Sarah emphasizes the importance of appreciating growth and transformation that come from facing adversity head-on. Challenges aren't roadblocks; they're opportunities for personal development, building resilience, and discovering more about ourselves. By recognizing and valuing these aspects, we can navigate life's twists and turns with grace and gratitude.

Chapter Explanation (Detailed):

Chapter 4, "Ugly Beautiful," is like a thrilling adventure into the heart of finding beauty and meaning in life's toughest challenges and adversities.

Sarah Jakes Roberts kicks off this exhilarating journey by introducing the concept of "ugly beautiful." It's as if she hands us a pair of magical glasses that allow us to see beauty where we might not have seen it before. This concept encourages us to shift our perspective and discover elements of beauty, growth, and transformation even in the midst of life's most challenging circumstances.

The chapter is all about embracing the idea that beauty can emerge from adversity. While facing difficult situations may bring discomfort and pain, it's also a powerful force for positive change. Sarah's like a coach, motivating us to look beyond the surface and uncover the silver linings and invaluable lessons that adversity holds. It's like finding a hidden treasure chest within the storm.

Furthermore, Sarah underlines the significance of appreciating the growth and transformation that adversity brings into our lives. Challenges aren't roadblocks; they're stepping stones on our journey to becoming the best version of ourselves. They're like the workout sessions for our personal development and resilience. By recognizing and cherishing these aspects, we can navigate life's ups and downs with a sense of poise and gratitude. It's like turning life's setbacks into powerful moments of self-discovery and strength-building.

Define in your own words what "ugly beautiful" means to you.

_____

_____

_____

_____

_____

_____

_____

_____

_____

_____

_____

_____

_____

_____

_____

_____

_____

_____

_____

_____

_____

_____

_____

_____

_____

_____

_____

_____

Describe a personal experience where you found beauty in a challenging situation.

_____

_____

_____

_____

_____

_____

_____

_____

_____

_____

_____

_____

_____

_____

_____

_____

_____

_____

_____

_____

_____

_____

_____

_____

_____

_____

_____

_____

Explain how changing your perspective can help you see the "ugly beautiful" in life's challenges.
Share a story of someone you know who embraced the concept of "ugly beautiful."

_____

_____

_____

_____

_____

_____

_____

_____

_____

_____

Cloze Tests:
"Ugly beautiful" encourages us to find beauty in the midst of life's
_____.
Changing our perspective can help us discover elements of
_____ and growth in challenging situations.
Define "ugly beautiful" as the ability to see _____ in adversity.
Embracing the concept of "ugly beautiful" is like putting on a new
pair of _____.
True/False Exercises:
True or False: "Ugly beautiful" is about ignoring the challenges in life.
True or False: Changing your perspective has no impact on finding
beauty in adversity.
True or False: "Ugly beautiful" means seeing beauty in challeng-
ing situations.
True or False: Embracing the concept of "ugly beautiful" is like
wearing magical glasses.

Lesson 2:

Embrace the idea that beauty can emerge from difficult situations.

Share a personal story of a time when you witnessed beauty emerging from adversity.

_____

_____

_____

_____

_____

_____

_____

_____

_____

_____

_____

_____

_____

_____

_____

_____

_____

_____

_____

_____

_____

_____

_____

_____

_____

_____

_____

_____

_____

List three qualities or characteristics that can develop as a result of facing difficult situations.

_____

_____

_____

_____

_____

_____

_____

_____

_____

_____

_____

_____

_____

_____

_____

_____

_____

_____

_____

_____

_____

_____

_____

_____

Reflect on how challenges have contributed to your personal growth and resilience. Describe a specific situation where you found beauty in a difficult circumstance.

_____

_____

_____

_____

_____

_____

_____

_____

_____

_____

Cloze Tests:

Adversity has the potential to give birth to _____.

Facing difficult situations can lead to the development of valuable _____.

Challenges contribute to our personal _____ and resilience.

Beauty can _____ from even the most challenging circumstances.

True/False Exercises:

True or False: Beauty can never emerge from difficult situations.

True or False: Facing challenges has no impact on personal growth.

True or False: Adversity can lead to the development of valuable qualities.

True or False: Finding beauty in difficult circumstances is impossible.

Lesson 3:

Learn to appreciate the growth and transformation that come from adversity.

Describe a challenge you faced that resulted in personal growth and transformation.

List three ways in which adversity has shaped your character.

_____
_____
_____
_____
_____
_____
_____
_____
_____
_____
_____
_____
_____
_____
_____
_____
_____
_____
_____
_____
_____
_____
_____
_____
_____
_____
_____
_____

Reflect on the importance of gratitude in recognizing the value of adversity. Share a personal story of someone who embraced adversity as an opportunity for growth.

_____

_____

_____

_____

_____

_____

_____

_____

_____

_____

_____

_____

Cloze Tests:

Adversity is like a workout session for our personal _____.

Challenges shape our _____ and character.

Gratitude plays a crucial role in recognizing the value of

_____.

Embracing adversity can lead to personal _____.

True/False Exercises:

True or False: Adversity has no impact on personal growth and transformation.

True or False: Challenges have no influence on character development.

True or False: Gratitude is irrelevant when it comes to recognizing the value of adversity.

True or False: Embracing adversity doesn't lead to personal development.

Chapter 5: When Forgiveness Meets Accountability

Welcome to Chapter 5 of "Woman Evolve: Break Up with Your Fears and Revolutionize Your Life" by Sarah Jakes Roberts! In this chapter, we're diving deep into the fascinating relationship between forgiveness and accountability.

Hold onto your hats because we're exploring the intersection of forgiveness and accountability. Sarah Jakes Roberts invites us to understand how true healing often involves a delicate balance of forgiving others and taking responsibility for our own actions and choices. It's like dancing on a tightrope of personal growth.

Get ready for the healing journey because this chapter highlights the incredible power of forgiveness. Whether it's forgiving others or forgiving ourselves, it's like unburdening ourselves from the weight of the past. Forgiveness creates space for personal growth and transformation, and it's a beautiful gift we give to ourselves.

Brace yourselves for the importance of taking responsibility for our actions and choices. Sarah emphasizes that accountability is a crucial aspect of personal development and self-improvement. It's like having a guiding compass that helps us make better choices and evolve as individuals.

Chapter Explanation (Detailed):

Chapter 5, "When Forgiveness Meets Accountability," is an exciting exploration of the intricate relationship between forgiveness and accountability.

Sarah Jakes Roberts kicks things off by inviting us to delve into the fascinating intersection of forgiveness and accountability. It's like embarking on a dance where we learn to balance forgiving others and holding ourselves accountable for our actions and choices. This chapter uncovers the delicate art of finding equilibrium in this transformative process.

The chapter spotlights the incredible healing power of forgiveness. Whether we're forgiving others or extending forgiveness to ourselves, it's like setting free the heavy baggage of the past. Forgiveness creates a spacious arena for emotional healing and personal growth, and it's a precious gift we offer ourselves in the journey towards self-discovery.

Furthermore, Sarah underlines the paramount importance of taking responsibility for our actions and choices. Accountability becomes our guiding star on the path of personal development and self-improvement. It's like having a compass that steers us towards making wiser decisions and evolving into better versions of ourselves.

What does the intersection of forgiveness and accountability mean to you? Can you provide an example from your life where forgiveness and accountability intersected?

Describe a situation where forgiveness without accountability might be ineffective. How can understanding the relationship between forgiveness and accountability benefit your personal growth?

_____
_____
_____
_____
_____
_____
_____
_____
_____
_____
_____
_____
_____
_____
_____
_____
_____
_____
_____
_____
_____
_____
_____
_____
_____
_____
_____

List three ways in which forgiveness and accountability can coexist harmoniously. Share a personal story of how acknowledging the intersection of forgiveness and accountability led to positive change in your life.

_____

_____

_____

_____

_____

_____

_____

_____

Cloze Tests:

Forgiveness and _____ are intertwined concepts.

The delicate balance between forgiving others and taking _____ is like a tightrope walk.

Understanding the relationship between forgiveness and _____ is crucial for personal growth.

Forgiveness creates space for emotional _____ and transformation.

Accountability is like a guiding _____ on the path of self-improvement.

Finding _____ in the process of forgiveness and accountability is an art.

True/False Exercises:

True or False: Forgiveness and accountability are completely separate concepts.

True or False: Understanding the relationship between forgiveness and accountability is unnecessary for personal development.

True or False: Forgiveness can lead to emotional healing and personal growth.

True or False: Accountability is not important on the path of self-improvement.

Lesson 2:

Understand the healing power of forgiving others and oneself:

How has forgiving others impacted your emotional well-being? Describe a situation where forgiving yourself was a catalyst for healing.

List three emotional benefits of forgiving others.
What steps can you take to practice self-forgiveness in your life?

_____

_____

_____

_____

_____

_____

_____

_____

_____

Share a personal story of how forgiveness led to healing in your
relationships.
How can forgiving both others and yourself contribute to your overall well-being?

_____

_____

_____

_____

_____

_____

_____

_____

_____

_____

_____

_____

Cloze Tests:

Forgiveness has the power to heal emotional
_____.

Self-forgiveness can be a catalyst for personal
_____.

Forgiving others can improve _____ well-being.

Practicing self-forgiveness involves being
_____ with oneself.

Share a personal story of how _____ contributed to healing in your life.

True/False Exercises:

True or False: Forgiveness has no impact on emotional healing.

True or False: Self-forgiveness is not important for personal growth.

True or False: Forgiving others can lead to an improvement in emotional well-being.

True or False: Practicing self-forgiveness means being overly critical of oneself.

True or False: Forgiveness always results in healing.

Lesson 3:

Learn how to take responsibility for your actions and choices:

Why is taking responsibility for your actions and choices essential for personal development? Describe a situation where taking responsibility for your choices led to positive outcomes.

_____

_____

_____

_____

_____

_____

_____

_____

_____

_____

_____

_____

_____

_____

_____

_____

_____

_____

_____

_____

_____

_____

_____

_____

_____

_____

_____

_____

List three ways in which accountability can help you make better decisions. What steps can you take to improve your ability to take responsibility in challenging situations?

_____

_____

_____

_____

_____

_____

_____

_____

_____

_____

_____

_____

_____

_____

_____

_____

_____

_____

_____

_____

_____

_____

_____

_____

_____

_____

Share a personal story of how embracing accountability transformed your life. How can taking responsibility for your actions and choices be a catalyst for self-improvement?

_____

_____

_____

_____

_____

_____

_____

_____

_____

Cloze Tests:

Taking responsibility for one's actions and choices is crucial for personal _____.

Embracing _____ can lead to better decision-making.

Accountability is like a _____ that guides us in making wiser choices.

Improving our ability to take _____ involves self-reflection.

Share a personal story of how _____ transformed your life.

True/False Exercises:

True or False: Taking responsibility for your actions and choices has no impact on personal development.

True or False: Accountability doesn't play a role in decision-making.

True or False: Accountability is like a guiding compass.

True or False: Improving accountability involves avoiding self-reflection.

True or False: Taking responsibility for one's actions and choices is essential for self-improvement.

Chapter 6: Black Women's Superpower

Buckle up, because we're diving into the incredible power of Black women. Sarah Jakes Roberts invites us to honor and recognize the extraordinary strengths and resilience that are often exclusive to Black women. It's time to shine a spotlight on the qualities and experiences that make them powerful and resilient.

Hold onto your hats, folks! We're about to explore the importance of sisterhood and community. This chapter drives home the message that Black women can find incredible strength, support, and inspiration by coming together. Sisterhood is more than a bond; it's a source of empowerment.

Get ready to discover your own superpowers! Sarah encourages all readers, no matter where you come from, to uncover and harness your unique strengths. It's about recognizing what makes you strong and resilient. This chapter provides insights and practical advice on how to use these superpowers to conquer life's challenges.

Chapter 6, "Black Women's Superpower," is an enthusiastic celebration and exploration of the exceptional strengths and resilience often found in Black women.

Sarah Jakes Roberts kicks things off by inviting us to celebrate and honor the remarkable strengths and resilience that are a defining feature of Black women. This chapter dives deep into the qualities and experiences that contribute to their extraordinary power. It's a reminder that diversity is a wellspring of strength, and Black women bring a unique and powerful perspective to the world.

The chapter also turns the spotlight on the vital role of sisterhood and community. It emphasizes how Black women can draw strength, support, and inspiration from one another. Sisterhood isn't just a connection; it's a wellspring of empowerment. This sense of community creates a nurturing environment for personal growth and resilience.

What are some unique strengths and qualities you associate with Black women? How can celebrating the resilience of Black women empower you in your own life?

Share a personal story of a Black woman who has inspired you with her strength. List three ways in which recognizing the strengths of Black women can promote diversity and inclusion.

_____

_____

_____

_____

_____

_____

_____

_____

_____

_____

_____

_____

_____

_____

_____

_____

_____

_____

_____

_____

_____

_____

_____

_____

_____

Describe a situation where you witnessed the resilience of a Black woman in your community. How can celebrating diversity of strengths among women benefit society as a whole?

_____

_____

_____

_____

_____

_____

_____

_____

_____

_____

Cloze Tests:

This chapter emphasizes celebrating the unique strengths and _____ of Black women.

Recognizing the resilience of Black women can be a source of _____ in your life.

Diversity and _____ are promoted when we acknowledge the strengths of Black women.

Share a personal story of a Black woman who has _____ you with her strength.

Celebrating the diversity of strengths among women can lead to a more _____ society.

True/False Exercises:

True or False: Black women do not possess unique strengths or qualities.

True or False: Recognizing the resilience of Black women has no impact on personal empowerment.

True or False: Acknowledging the strengths of Black women promotes diversity and inclusion.

True or False: Black women's strength is not relevant to society as a whole.

True or False: Celebrating diversity of strengths among women is important for a harmonious society.

Lesson 2:

Recognize the importance of sisterhood and community:

How has sisterhood or community support played a role in your personal growth? Describe a specific instance where you experienced the power of sisterhood or community.

List three benefits of being part of a supportive sisterhood or community. What steps can individuals take to foster a sense of community and sisterhood in their lives?

_____

_____

_____

_____

_____

_____

_____

_____

_____

_____

_____

_____

_____

_____

_____

_____

_____

_____

_____

_____

_____

_____

_____

_____

Share a personal story of how sisterhood or community support helped you overcome a challenge. How can sisterhood and community support lead to empowerment?

_____

_____

_____

_____

_____

_____

_____

_____

_____

Cloze Tests:

This chapter highlights the significance of _____ and community.

Being part of a supportive sisterhood or community can provide numerous _____.

Fostering a sense of _____ is essential for personal growth.

Share a personal story of how _____ support helped you overcome a challenge.

Sisterhood and community support are powerful sources of _____.

True/False Exercises:

True or False: Sisterhood and community support have no impact on personal growth.

True or False: There are no benefits to being part of a supportive sisterhood or community.

True or False: Fostering a sense of community is irrelevant to personal development.

True or False: Sisterhood and community support cannot help individuals overcome challenges.

True or False: Sisterhood and community support are not sources of empowerment.

Lesson 3:

Harness your own superpowers to overcome obstacles:

What do you consider your unique superpowers or strengths?
Describe a situation where you used your superpowers to overcome
a significant obstacle.

List three strategies you can employ to better harness your superpowers in challenging times.
How can recognizing your superpowers boost your self-confidence?

_____

_____

_____

_____

_____

_____

_____

_____

_____

_____

_____

_____

_____

_____

_____

_____

_____

_____

_____

_____

_____

_____

Share a personal story of someone who inspired you by harnessing their unique strengths.
How can harnessing your superpowers lead to personal growth and resilience?

_____

_____

_____

_____

_____

_____

_____

_____

Cloze Tests:
This chapter encourages readers to _____ their unique superpowers.
Using your superpowers to overcome obstacles can be a source of _____.

Strategies for better harnessing your superpowers include _____.

Recognizing your superpowers can boost your _____.
Share a personal story of someone who inspired you by _____ their unique strengths.

True/False Exercises:
True or False: Everyone possesses unique superpowers or strengths.
True or False: Using your superpowers to overcome obstacles has no impact on personal growth.
True or False: Recognizing your superpowers can boost your self-confidence.
True or False: Harnessing your superpowers is unrelated to personal growth and resilience.
True or False: Others cannot inspire you by harnessing their unique strengths.

Chapter 7: Love in the Layers

Buckle up, because in Chapter 7 of "Woman Evolve: Break Up with Your Fears and Revolutionize Your Life" by Sarah Jakes Roberts, we're diving deep into the fascinating and complex world of love and its impact on our lives.

Get ready to explore the multifaceted nature of love and relationships. Sarah Jakes Roberts encourages us to embrace the idea that love is not a one-size-fits-all concept; it's beautifully diverse and intricate. This chapter sparks a curiosity to dig deeper and understand what love truly means in various aspects of our lives.

Hold onto your hats, folks, because we're about to dive into the layers of love. Love isn't limited to romantic relationships; it's a multi-dimensional force that touches self-love, family love, friendships, and so much more. Each layer of love brings its own unique qualities and significance, and it's time to uncover their hidden treasures.

Get ready to be transformed! Sarah emphasizes the incredible power of love to heal, inspire, and bring about positive change. Love isn't just a feeling; it's a force that can lead us on a journey of personal growth and inner transformation. This chapter is a celebration of the potential for love to be a catalyst for positive change in our lives.

Chapter Explanation (Detailed):

Chapter 7, "Love in the Layers," takes us on an exciting journey into the multifaceted world of love and its profound influence on our lives.

Sarah Jakes Roberts kicks things off by inviting us to embrace the idea that love is wonderfully complex and diverse. It's not a one-size-fits-all concept; it can take on various forms and intricacies. This chapter sparks our curiosity to explore what love truly means to us in different contexts. It's an invitation to dive beneath the surface and discover that love isn't always straightforward; its complexity enriches our understanding of it.

The chapter also encourages us to explore the layers of love in various aspects of our lives. Love isn't confined to romantic relationships; it extends to self-love, love for family, friendship, community, and beyond. Each layer of love brings its own unique qualities and significance, much like uncovering hidden treasures. By delving into these layers, we gain a richer appreciation for the depth and diversity of love in our lives.

What does love mean to you, and how has it evolved in your life?
Describe a complex or multifaceted aspect of a past or current relationship.

List three factors that contribute to the complexity of love and relationships.
How can understanding the complexity of love enhance your ability to navigate relationships?

_____

_____

_____

_____

_____

_____

_____

_____

_____

_____

_____

_____

_____

_____

_____

_____

_____

_____

_____

_____

_____

_____

_____

Share a personal story of a relationship that taught you about the intricate nature of love. Explain the importance of open communication in dealing with complex relationship dynamics.

_____

_____

_____

_____

_____

_____

_____

_____

Cloze Tests:

This chapter encourages us to understand the _____ of love and relationships.

Love can be _____ and multifaceted.

Factors contributing to the complexity of love and relationships include _____.

Understanding the complexity of love can improve your _____ in relationships.

Share a personal story of a _____ that taught you about the intricate nature of love.

Open _____ is crucial in navigating complex relationship dynamics.

True/False Exercises:

True or False: Love is a simple and straightforward emotion.

True or False: Relationships are always easy to navigate without any complexity.

True or False: Understanding the complexity of love is irrelevant in relationships.

True or False: Open communication is not important in dealing with complex relationships.

True or False: Love and relationships can be multifaceted and evolving.

True or False: Factors contributing to the complexity of love and relationships are varied.

Lesson 2:

Explore the layers of love in various aspects of life:

Identify and describe three different layers of love in your life (e.g., family, friendships, self-love).
How does the experience of love differ in various aspects of your life?

_____

_____

_____

_____

_____

_____

_____

_____

_____

_____

_____

_____

_____

_____

_____

_____

_____

_____

_____

_____

_____

_____

_____

_____

List three ways in which exploring different layers of love can enrich your understanding of it.
Share a personal story of a moment when you felt the depth of love in a non-romantic relationship.

_____

_____

_____

_____

_____

_____

_____

_____

_____

_____

_____

_____

_____

_____

_____

_____

_____

_____

_____

_____

_____

_____

_____

How can understanding the layers of love improve your overall well-being? Explain why self-love is a crucial layer of love to explore and nurture.

_____

_____

_____

_____

_____

_____

_____

_____

_____

_____

Cloze Tests:

This chapter encourages us to explore the _____ of love.

Love is not limited to _____ relationships.

Exploring different layers of love can _____ our understanding of it.

Share a personal story of a moment when you felt the depth of love in a _____ relationship.

Understanding the layers of love can have a positive impact on your _____.

True/False Exercises:

True or False: Love is only relevant in romantic relationships.

True or False: Exploring different layers of love does not enhance understanding.

True or False: Self-love is not an important aspect of love.

True or False: Understanding the layers of love can impact overall well-being.

True or False: Love exists in various aspects of life beyond romantic relationships.

True or False: Exploring different layers of love enriches understanding.

Lesson 3:

Embrace the transformative power of love:

How has love transformed or changed you in your life?
Describe a situation where love played a transformative role in your
personal growth.

_____

_____

_____

_____

_____

_____

_____

_____

_____

_____

_____

_____

_____

_____

_____

_____

_____

_____

_____

_____

_____

_____

_____

_____

_____

List three ways in which love can be a catalyst for positive change. How can you harness the transformative power of love in your daily life?

_____

_____

_____

_____

_____

_____

_____

_____

_____

_____

_____

_____

_____

_____

_____

_____

_____

_____

_____

_____

_____

_____

_____

_____

Share a personal story of someone whose life was positively transformed by love. Explain why self-love is a fundamental aspect of personal transformation through love.

_____

_____

_____

_____

_____

_____

_____

_____

_____

_____

Cloze Tests:

This chapter emphasizes embracing the _____ of love.

Love has the potential to be a _____ for personal growth.

Love can be a catalyst for positive _____.

Harnessing the transformative power of love involves _____.

Share a personal story of someone whose life was positively _____ by love.

Self-love is a fundamental aspect of personal _____ through love.

True/False Exercises:

True or False: Love has no transformative power.

True or False: Love cannot be a catalyst for positive change.

True or False: Embracing the transformative power of love is irrelevant.

True or False: Self-love is not important for personal transformation through love.

True or False: Love has the potential to positively impact personal growth.

True or False: Love can be a force for positive change.

Chapter 8: The Great Envy

In Chapter 8 of "Woman Evolve: Break Up with Your Fears and Revolutionize Your Life" by Sarah Jakes Roberts, we're diving headfirst into the deep waters of envy. It's a pervasive issue that can really mess with our well-being and personal growth, so let's break it down and find ways to overcome it.

Confronting Envy and Comparison: First up, Sarah Jakes Roberts wants us to take a good, hard look at envy and comparison in our own lives. Envy often creeps in when we start comparing ourselves to others, right? It's like this sneaky little monster that can hold us back from growing and being happy. This chapter is all about turning that flashlight inward and getting real about how envy might be messing with our mojo.

Envy as a Hindrance: Envy can be a major roadblock on our path to personal growth and happiness. Think about it—when we're constantly sizing ourselves up against others and wishing we had what they have, it can make us feel inadequate and unhappy. Recognizing this negative impact is the first step toward getting rid of envy's grip on us.

Cultivating Gratitude and Contentment: So, how do we shake off envy's tight hold? Sarah's got some wisdom to share. It's all about cultivating gratitude and contentment. Gratitude is like a magic wand that shifts our focus from what we don't have to what we do, creating a sense of abundance and appreciation. Contentment lets us find peace and fulfillment in the here and now, instead of constantly chasing after things we think will make us happy. This chapter is packed with practical tips to help us nurture these qualities in our lives.

Have you ever experienced envy or comparison in your life? Describe a specific situation. How do envy and comparison affect your personal well-being and happiness?

_____

_____

_____

_____

_____

_____

_____

_____

_____

_____

_____

_____

_____

_____

_____

_____

_____

_____

_____

_____

_____

_____

_____

_____

List three negative consequences of constantly comparing yourself to others. Share a personal story of someone who overcame envy and comparison in their life.

_____
_____
_____
_____
_____
_____
_____
_____
_____
_____
_____
_____
_____
_____
_____
_____
_____
_____
_____
_____
_____
_____
_____
_____
_____

What strategies can you employ to address and overcome envy when it arises? Explain the difference between healthy competition and destructive envy.

_____

_____

_____

_____

_____

_____

_____

_____

_____

Cloze Tests:

Chapter 8 encourages us to address the issue of _____ and comparison.

Envy often creeps in when we start _____ ourselves to others.

Comparing ourselves to others can hold us back from _____ and happiness.

Share a personal story of someone who _____ envy and comparison in their life.

Overcoming envy involves employing _____ strategies.

Healthy competition differs from destructive _____.

True/False Exercises:

True or False: Envy and comparison have no impact on personal well-being.

True or False: Envy and comparison can be positive motivators.

True or False: Comparing oneself to others always leads to happiness.

True or False: Addressing envy involves recognizing its presence in your life.

True or False: Healthy competition and destructive envy are the same.

True or False: Envy never holds us back from personal growth.

Lesson 2:

Recognize that envy can hinder personal growth and happiness:

How has envy hindered your personal growth or happiness in the past? List three ways in which envy can negatively impact your relationships with others.

Share a personal story of someone who struggled with envy and its consequences. What steps can individuals take to recognize envy's negative influence in their lives?

_____

_____

_____

_____

_____

_____

_____

_____

_____

_____

_____

_____

_____

_____

_____

_____

_____

_____

_____

_____

_____

_____

_____

_____

Describe a situation where envy prevented you from pursuing your goals or dreams. Explain why self-awareness is crucial in recognizing envy's hindrance to personal growth.

_____

_____

_____

_____

_____

_____

_____

_____

_____

Cloze Tests:

Envy can be a major _____ to personal growth and happiness.

Envy negatively impacts our _____ with others.

Share a personal story of someone who struggled with envy and its

_____.

Recognizing envy's negative _____ is the first step in overcoming it.

Envy can hinder individuals from pursuing their _____ or dreams.

Self-_____ is crucial in recognizing envy's hindrance to personal growth.

True/False Exercises:

True or False: Envy never hinders personal growth or happiness.

True or False: Envy has a positive impact on relationships with others.

True or False: Recognizing envy's negative influence is not important.

True or False: Envy can prevent individuals from pursuing their goals or dreams.

True or False: Self-awareness plays a crucial role in recognizing envy's hindrance.

Lesson 3:

Cultivate gratitude and contentment to overcome envy:

How do gratitude and contentment differ from envy?
Describe a situation where practicing gratitude helped you overcome envy.

List three daily practices that can help you cultivate gratitude. Explain the role of contentment in reducing the grip of envy in your life.

_____

_____

_____

_____

_____

_____

_____

_____

_____

_____

_____

_____

_____

_____

_____

_____

_____

_____

_____

_____

_____

_____

_____

_____

Share a personal story of someone who transformed their life by embracing gratitude and contentment.
How can the practice of gratitude and contentment lead to personal growth and happiness?

_____

_____

_____

_____

_____

_____

_____

Cloze Tests:

Overcoming envy involves cultivating _____ and contentment.

Gratitude shifts our focus from what we don't have to what we _____.

Daily practices like keeping a gratitude _____ can help nurture gratitude.

Contentment allows us to find _____ and fulfillment in the present.

Share a personal story of someone who transformed their life by embracing _____ and contentment.

The practice of gratitude and contentment can lead to _____ growth and happiness.

True/False Exercises:

True or False: Gratitude and contentment are synonymous with envy.

True or False: Practicing gratitude has no impact on reducing envy.

True or False: Daily practices cannot help nurture gratitude.

True or False: Contentment is unrelated to personal growth and happiness.

True or False: Embracing gratitude and contentment can transform one's life.

True or False: Gratitude and contentment have no impact on personal growth.

Chapter 9: Leaving Pieces Behind

Chapter 9 in "Woman Evolve: Break Up with Your Fears and Revolutionize Your Life" by Sarah Jakes Roberts is an exciting journey into the realm of personal growth and transformation. Let's dive into the key takeaways and lessons with enthusiasm:

Exploring What No Longer Serves You: Sarah Jakes Roberts encourages us to embark on a thrilling exploration of what no longer serves us. It's like spring cleaning for your life! This means taking a close look at our habits, relationships, beliefs, and patterns that might be holding us back. By identifying and letting go of what doesn't align with our growth and well-being, we make space for fresh and positive experiences.

Shedding Old Patterns and Beliefs: In this captivating chapter, we discover the importance of shedding old patterns and beliefs that no longer serve us. Think of it as shedding old skin to reveal the vibrant new you underneath. Sometimes, we hold onto outdated ways of thinking and behaving that keep us stuck. Sarah encourages us to break free from these limitations and open ourselves up to new possibilities, like turning a new page in the book of our lives.

Embracing Personal Evolution: At the heart of this chapter lies the thrilling idea of embracing personal evolution. Life is an exciting adventure filled with change and transformation. Sarah reminds us that it's perfectly okay to outgrow certain aspects of our past selves. Embracing personal evolution means accepting that we are constantly evolving and that our journey may take us to unexpected and exciting destinations. It's all about confidently stepping into the fullness of who we are becoming

Can you identify one habit in your life that you believe no longer serves your personal growth?
How does letting go of what no longer serves you create space for positive experiences?

_____

_____

_____

_____

_____

_____

_____

_____

_____

_____

_____

_____

_____

_____

_____

_____

_____

_____

_____

_____

_____

_____

_____

_____

List three areas in your life where you feel you might need to leave behind something that's holding you back.
Share a personal story of a time when you successfully left behind something that wasn't serving your well-being.

_____

_____

_____

_____

_____

_____

_____

_____

_____

_____

_____

_____

_____

_____

_____

_____

_____

_____

_____

_____

_____

_____

_____

What emotional benefits can come from the process of leaving behind what no longer serves you?
Explain the importance of periodically reassessing your life to identify what needs to be left behind.

_____

_____

_____

_____

_____

_____

_____

Cloze Tests:

Chapter 9 encourages us to explore the concept of leaving behind what no longer _____ us.

Letting go of what no longer serves you creates space for _____ experiences.

Areas in your life where you need to leave behind something that's holding you back are often _____.

Share a personal story of a time when you successfully _____ something that wasn't serving your well-being.

The process of leaving behind what no longer serves you can bring emotional _____.

Periodically reassessing your life is important to identify what needs to be left _____.

True/False Exercises:

True or False: Leaving behind what no longer serves you has no impact on personal growth.

True or False: Letting go of what doesn't serve you does not create space for positive experiences.

True or False: Identifying areas in your life that need change is irrelevant to personal growth.

True or False: Emotional benefits can come from the process of leaving behind what no longer serves you.

True or False: Reassessing your life periodically is unnecessary for personal growth.

Lesson 2:

Understand the importance of shedding old patterns and beliefs:

Can you identify one old pattern or belief in your life that you believe is holding you back? How does shedding old patterns and beliefs open up possibilities for personal growth?

List three ways in which old patterns and beliefs can limit your potential. Share a personal story of someone who transformed their life by shedding an old limiting belief.

_____

_____

_____

_____

_____

_____

_____

_____

_____

_____

_____

_____

_____

_____

_____

_____

_____

_____

_____

_____

_____

_____

_____

What steps can individuals take to break free from old patterns and beliefs that hinder them? Explain the connection between shedding old patterns and beliefs and personal empowerment.

_____

_____

_____

_____

_____

_____

_____

Cloze Tests:

Chapter 9 emphasizes the importance of shedding old _____ and beliefs.

Shedding old patterns and beliefs opens up _____ for personal growth.

Old patterns and beliefs can _____ your potential in multiple ways.

Share a personal story of someone who transformed their life by shedding an old _____ belief.

Breaking free from old patterns and beliefs that hinder you involves taking _____ steps.

Shedding old patterns and beliefs is closely related to personal _____.

True/False Exercises:

True or False: Shedding old patterns and beliefs has no impact on personal growth.

True or False: Old patterns and beliefs do not limit one's potential.

True or False: Breaking free from old patterns and beliefs is unnecessary for personal growth.

True or False: Shedding old patterns and beliefs is unrelated to personal empowerment.

True or False: Shedding old patterns and beliefs opens up possibilities for personal growth.

True or False: Transformation through shedding old beliefs is not achievable.

Lesson 3:

Embrace the process of personal evolution and growth:

How do you personally define the concept of personal evolution? Share a specific example of a time when you felt like you were embracing personal evolution.

_____

_____

_____

_____

_____

_____

_____

_____

_____

_____

_____

_____

_____

_____

_____

_____

_____

_____

_____

_____

_____

_____

_____

_____

_____

_____

_____

List three benefits of wholeheartedly embracing personal evolution and growth.
What challenges or fears might individuals face when trying to embrace personal evolution?

_____

_____

_____

_____

_____

_____

_____

_____

_____

_____

_____

_____

_____

_____

_____

_____

_____

_____

_____

_____

_____

_____

_____

Describe a situation where personal growth resulted in a positive change in someone's life.
How can embracing personal evolution lead to a more fulfilling life?

_____

_____

_____

_____

_____

_____

_____

_____

Cloze Tests:
This chapter encourages us to embrace the process of personal _____ and growth.
Embracing personal evolution often involves stepping out of your _____ zone.
Benefits of embracing personal evolution and growth are _____.
Facing challenges and fears is common when individuals try to embrace personal _____.
Personal growth can result in positive _____ in one's life.
Embracing personal evolution can lead to a more _____ life.
True/False Exercises:
True or False: Embracing personal evolution has no impact on personal growth.
True or False: Embracing personal evolution does not require stepping out of one's comfort zone.
True or False: Personal growth does not lead to positive changes in life.
True or False: Embracing personal evolution is unrelated to a fulfilling life.
True or False: Benefits of embracing personal evolution and growth are varied.
True or False: Facing challenges and fears is uncommon when individuals embrace personal evolution.

Chapter 10: Revolutionizing Your Life

Chapter 10, "Revolutionizing Your Life," serves as the crescendo of our incredible journey through "Woman Evolve: Break Up with Your Fears and Revolutionize Your Life" by Sarah Jakes Roberts. As we delve into the key takeaways and lessons, we're going to channel an infectious enthusiasm, ready to empower ourselves and create positive change:

Main Lessons and Takeaways:

Take Action to Revolutionize Your Life: Sarah Jakes Roberts ignites our motivation to take dynamic action and revolutionize our lives, unlocking our full potential. It's like revving up the engine of your dream car; you have the power to steer your life in the direction you desire. This chapter encourages us to rise above the ordinary, urging us not to settle but to actively chase our dreams and ambitions.

Embrace Change and Transformation as a Continuous Journey: The chapter reminds us that change and transformation aren't one-time pit stops but a thrilling, ongoing journey. Picture it like a roller-coaster ride where every twist and turn propels you toward growth and self-discovery. Embrace the idea that life is an ever-evolving process, a continuous opportunity to reshape yourself.

Empower Yourself to Break Free from Limitations and Fears: Sarah empowers us to shatter the shackles of limitations and fears that may have held us back. Visualize it as stepping into the sunlight after being in the shadows for too long. This chapter equips us with practical tools and strategies to confront and conquer the fears and doubts that have hindered our progress. It's like having a coach cheering you on as you conquer your fears.

What does taking dynamic action to revolutionize your life mean to you? Share a specific goal or dream you want to achieve and the actions you plan to take to get there.

List three ways in which taking action can help you unlock your full potential. Describe a personal experience where taking action led to a positive change in your life.

_____

_____

_____

_____

_____

_____

_____

_____

_____

_____

_____

_____

_____

_____

_____

_____

_____

_____

_____

_____

_____

_____

_____

How can individuals stay motivated and consistent in taking action toward their goals? Explain why settling for mediocrity is not an option if you want to revolutionize your life.

_____

_____

_____

_____

_____

_____

_____

_____

Cloze Tests:

Chapter 10 inspires us to take action to revolutionize our lives and reach our full _____.

Taking dynamic action means having the power to steer your life in the direction you _____.

Taking action can help you unlock your full potential and chase your dreams and _____.

Taking action often leads to positive _____ in one's life.

Staying motivated and consistent in taking action involves finding sources of _____.

Settling for mediocrity is not an _____ if you want to revolutionize your life.

True/False Exercises:

True or False: Taking action has no impact on unlocking one's full potential.

True or False: Settling for mediocrity is a valid option in life.

True or False: Taking action means surrendering control of your life.

True or False: Staying motivated and consistent in taking action is unnecessary.

True or False: Taking action can lead to positive changes in life.

True or False: Chasing your dreams and aspirations requires no effort.

Lesson 2:

Embrace change and transformation as a continuous journey:

How do you personally view change and transformation as a continuous journey? Share an example of a recent change or transformation in your life and how it impacted you.

_____
_____
_____
_____
_____
_____
_____
_____
_____
_____
_____
_____
_____
_____
_____
_____
_____
_____
_____
_____
_____
_____
_____
_____
_____
_____
_____

List three benefits of embracing change and transformation as an ongoing process. Describe a situation where resisting change hindered personal growth or happiness.

_____

_____

_____

_____

_____

_____

_____

_____

_____

_____

_____

_____

_____

_____

_____

_____

_____

_____

_____

_____

_____

_____

_____

_____

What mindset shift is necessary to fully embrace change and transformation in life? Explain why life is often compared to an ever-evolving journey of growth and self-discovery.

_____

_____

_____

_____

_____

_____

_____

Cloze Tests:

This chapter encourages us to embrace change and transformation as an ongoing _____.

Change and transformation are like a thrilling adventure with no final _____.

Embracing change and transformation brings multiple

_____.

Resisting change can hinder personal _____ or happiness.

Fully embracing change and transformation requires a _____ shift.

Life is often compared to an ever-evolving journey of _____ and self-discovery.

True/False Exercises:

True or False: Change and transformation are solitary events with final destinations.

True or False: Embracing change and transformation has no benefits.

True or False: Resisting change always leads to personal growth and happiness.

True or False: Life is not comparable to an ever-evolving journey.

True or False: Embracing change and transformation requires no mindset shift.

True or False: Change and transformation have no impact on self-discovery.

Lesson 3:

Empower yourself to break free from limitations and fears:

Share a personal fear or limitation that you want to break free from.
Describe a time when you overcame a significant fear and how it
impacted your life.

List three strategies or techniques that can help individuals conquer their fears. How can empowering yourself to break free from limitations lead to personal growth?

_____

_____

_____

_____

_____

_____

_____

_____

_____

_____

_____

_____

_____

_____

_____

_____

_____

_____

_____

_____

_____

_____

_____

_____

Explain the role of self-confidence in confronting and overcoming limitations. Share a story of someone who empowered themselves to break free from a major limitation.

_____

_____

_____

_____

_____

_____

_____

_____

Cloze Tests:
The chapter empowers us to break free from limitations and

_____.

Overcoming a significant fear can have a profound impact on one's

_____.

Strategies and techniques can be employed to conquer _____.
Empowering yourself to break free from limitations can pave the way for personal _____.
Self-confidence plays a crucial role in confronting and overcoming

_____.

Share a story of someone who empowered themselves to break free from a major _____.

True/False Exercises:
True or False: Breaking free from limitations and fears has no impact on personal growth.
True or False: Conquering fears requires no strategies or techniques.
True or False: Self-confidence is irrelevant in confronting and overcoming limitations.
True or False: Empowering oneself to break free from limitations is unattainable.
True or False: Overcoming a significant fear has no impact on one's life.
True or False: Limitations and fears cannot be conquered.

Made in the USA
Columbia, SC
03 October 2024

43561000R00070